THE GIFT OF THE
ANOINTING OF THE SICK

THE GIFT OF THE ANOINTING OF THE SICK

A PREPARATION GUIDE FOR THE SACRAMENT

MARY KATHLEEN GLAVICH, SND

acta
PUBLICATIONS

THE GIFT OF THE ANOINTING OF THE SICK
A Preparation Guide for the Sacrament
Mary Kathleen Glavich, SND

Edited by Gregory F. A. Pierce
Cover design by Tom A. Wright
Text Design and typesetting by Patricia A. Lynch

Published by ACTA Publications, 5559 W. Howard Street, Skokie, IL 60077
(800) 397-2282 www.actapublications.com.

Library of Congress Number: 2006925714
ISBN 10: 0-87946-310-4
ISBN 13: 978-0-87946-310-6
Printed in the United States of America
Year: 15 14 13 12 10 9 8 7 6
Printing: 10 9 8 7 6 5 4 3 2 1

CONTENTS

When this perishable body puts on imperishability, and this mortal body puts on immortality, then the saying that is written will be fulfilled:

"Death has been swallowed up in victory."
"Where, O death, is your victory?
Where, O death, is your sting?"

The sting of death is sin, and the power of sin is the law. But thanks be to God, who gives us the victory through our Lord Jesus Christ.

I Corinthians 15:53–57

A SACRAMENT FOR HEALING

DEAR READER,

If you are reading this book, it is most likely because you or your loved one is about to receive the Sacrament of the Anointing of the Sick, either individually or in a communal setting. This book is meant to prepare you for receiving that sacrament.

Prior to the Second Vatican Council, the Sacrament of the Anointing of the Sick was commonly called "Extreme Unction," and ordinarily it was administered only when a person was actually dying and all hope for recovery was gone. Consequently it tended to be something to fear and avoid, almost as if it were "the kiss of death." Now the Anointing of the Sick has become a welcome and consoling event—a striking way that the Church supports and intercedes for those who are sick. In the process of bringing the Church up to date on many fronts, Vatican II also gave the "sacrament of the sick" an "extreme makeover."

By changing the name, reasons, rites and occasions for the Sacrament of the Anointing of the Sick, the Church actually restored it to its original form. Now this sacrament is more clearly an extension of the healing ministry of Jesus. It is a way we can experience his comfort and healing today and show support and love to our fellow Christians whenever they are seriously ill.

Because the Anointing of the Sick was usually part of the Last Rites—along with the sacrament of Penance (the other healing sacrament) and *Viaticum* (the Latin word for what is expected to be our final Communion)—the Anointing of the Sick came to be regarded as a last chance to squeeze through heaven's gates. Today the Anointing of the Sick is not meant to be the last sacrament received but rather a ritual of compassion that can be performed whenever anyone becomes gravely ill. The emphasis today is on the Anointing of the Sick's potential to strengthen us during illness, give us hope, and possibly even cure us if that is the divine will.

For example, many parishes occasionally offer the sacrament of the Anointing of the Sick during a communal celebration. At the priest's invitation people stream down the aisles, hoping to be healed. This was unheard of in modern times until the Second Vatican Council.

You may be puzzled or curious by these changes. You or your loved one may be hesitant to receive this anointing at times when it could do a world of good. You may not be sure exactly when to ask for the sacrament of the Anointing of the Sick or how to prepare for or celebrate it. If any or all of these are true, then this book is for you.

In these pages you will discover the beauty of the sacrament of the Anointing of the Sick as a celebration of faith. You will learn its history, the meaning of its symbols, the different ways it may be carried out, and its effects—both physical and spiritual. You will come to understand that through the sacrament of the Anointing of the Sick we experience the healing touch of Jesus, the Divine Physician, and know his love.

Sister Mary Kathleen Glavich, SND

HELP FOR A HURTING WORLD

Health, wholeness, holiness—these three words are related. They are the ideal we all strive for. The Bible says that when we were created, God saw that we were "very good." God had great dreams for us: We would live forever, sharing his life and love, and be holy and happy.

Then came the nightmare. Our first parents, whom we call Adam and Eve, committed the original sin, shattering their friendship with God and allowing evil to enter the world. Ever since then, human beings and our planet-home have been "sick." We are now imperfect beings in an imperfect world. We get headaches and colds, cancer and AIDS. We are proud and selfish, mean and dishonest. We fight wars and commit acts of terrorism and inhumanity on one another. Earth itself suffers natural disasters, some caused by our failure to care for the environment.

God, however, has not given up on us but constantly works toward making us healthy, whole and holy—even to the point of sending his Son to conquer evil and repair our relationship with God and with one another. By sharing our human condition, by suffering and dying, Jesus overcame sin and death. We say he won for us salvation, a word derived from the Latin *salus*, which means "health." In all that he did, Jesus carried out his self-proclaimed mission: "I have come that they may have life, and have it abundantly" (John 10:10).

JESUS THE HEALER

Jesus both announced and initiated God's kingdom. During public ministry in Israel, he demonstrated his power over evil by many forms of healing: He calmed storms and cast out devils; he healed people by forgiving their sins and giving them a new lease on life; he cured the blind, the lame, the deaf, paralyzed people and lepers. All were healed by his

What was visible in the Lord
has passed over into the sacraments.

Pope Leo the Great

touch. Jesus even brought people back to life.

Much of Jesus' time was spent healing. Why? Because healing is at the heart of the work of redemption. His final triumph over evil was achieved through his suffering, death, and rising to new life. Because of this "Paschal Mystery," all of us are saved, all of us are healed, and all of us can look forward to eternal life. We have Jesus' word for it.

MIRACLES HAPPEN EVERY DAY

Miracles of healing take place every day. It is part of the establishment of God's kingdom "on earth, as it is in heaven," as Jesus taught us to pray. It is a kingdom that is paradoxically already begun but not yet realized.

Every time that a doctor or nurse treats a patient, Jesus is there. Every time a researcher makes a discovery that might lead to the discovery of a vaccine or a new medicine, Jesus is carrying out his mission. Every time that a caregiver eases a loved one's pain, Jesus heals.

Jesus did not retire. Instead he handed on his ministry to his apostles, so that through his Church and its sacraments he could continue to do good and fight evil. The redemption of the world goes on. Jesus heals broken spirits through the Sacrament of Penance, and he heals broken bodies, minds and hearts through the Sacrament of the Anointing of the Sick.

God's compassion for the sick is shown in nonsacramental ways too. Shrines like Lourdes in France or Fatima in Portugal are famous for unexplainable cures that occur for pilgrims to them. Many saints are known for their ministering to the sick, and some saints and holy people (such as Brother André Besette and Father Solanus Casey) were blessed with the gift of healing. Certain religious communities founded to care for the sick began the enterprise of hospitals. Recently the charismatic movement arose, in which healing—a charismatic gift of the Holy Spirit—is a primary component.

Impetus for concern for the sick is given by Jesus' identity with them. He said, "I was sick and you took care of me" (Matthew 25:36). For his followers, visiting the sick is a corporal work of mercy, that is, a ticket to heaven. Through Jesus and the compassion of his Church, God constantly proves his words, "For surely I know the plans I have for you, says the LORD, plans for your welfare and not for harm, to give you a future with hope" (Jeremiah 29:11). Our God continues to show tender care for us.

THE EFFICACY OF SUFFERING

Illness, pain, and suffering are not good. These evils should not be simply endured but combated. This doesn't mean that suffering has no benefits. On the contrary, illness may lead a person to conversion of heart. Also the sick remind the rest of us that life is fragile and fleeting and that we'd better keep higher things in mind. God never fails to draw good out of evil.

Someone might ask about a sick person, "What did he or she do to deserve this?" But our God is not an "ambush" god. He does not dole out sickness or any other kind of evil as punishment for an individual sinner. Jesus dispelled that notion, which was common among the people of his time, even as it persists among many people today.

However you look at it, suffering remains a great mystery. In Scripture, when his unjust suffering puzzled Job, the only answer he received from God was this: Who are you to question the almighty creator? Because of Jesus, however, Christians can take suffering to another level. He truly is our "Wounded Healer," and by accepting our cross and uniting our suffering with his, we can join in his saving work. Our suffering too becomes redemptive. Patiently endured, it can make up for our sins as well as the sins of others. In this light, our suffering is not meaningless but can become fruitful, even if there is nothing else we have to offer. Closer union with Jesus in his suffering and death is a special and important vocation, in and of itself.

In my Father's house there are many dwelling places. If it were not so, would I have told you that I go to prepare a place for you? And if I go and prepare a place for you, I will come again and will take you to myself, so that where I am, there you may be also.

John 14:2–3

ONE OF THE SEVEN SACRAMENTS

A friend of mine named Ann was facing double surgery. To repair a herniated disk she was going to have a piece of her hip removed and placed in her neck. Although she was forty-nine years old, she had never had a regular doctor, because she had always enjoyed good health. Ann was scared, and a week before the scheduled surgery she asked a priest for the Sacrament of the Anointing of the Sick. In a private chapel in the hospital he anointed her, just prior to her operation.

Ann had been warned to expect great pain after the procedure. Consequently, she lay awake following surgery, prepared to ask for medication immediately, but the pain never came. The next day, she was walking around the hospital without a walker or cane, and she was sent home that afternoon wearing a large neck brace. Some people suggested, "Perhaps you didn't feel any pain because you've become so used to pain that you don't recognize it." Others commented, "You must have a high tolerance level." Ann's doctor took credit, saying that he had perfected his medical techniques. Ann, though, felt that the Anointing of the Sick she had received had a lot to do with her experience.

No one can promise that the Anointing of the Sick will lesson your pain or that of your loved one. Nor will it guarantee a return to health or even a postponement of death. What the sacrament does—like all the sacraments do—is give you the grace to align yourself with God's will and open you to receiving God's grace, which is always abundant and available and free.

You might recall the traditional definition of a sacrament: an outward sign instituted by Christ to give grace. The Anointing of the Sick fits this description. The visible, sensible elements of a sacrament both express and bring about the invisible effects. Through outward signs of oil and the laying on of hands and a priest's words, the Anointing of the

Sick makes present in a real and special way God's life and power. Each sacrament imparts the grace unique to it. In the case of the Anointing of the Sick, it is the grace of healing.

AN ACT OF JESUS

Like any sacrament, the Anointing of the Sick is an encounter with Jesus. In it he acts to heal, just as he healed 2,000 years ago. The healing can be physical, mental or spiritual. It can be dramatic, such as a return to health, or scarcely noticeable, such as an inner healing of the heart. Through the signs and words of this sacrament, Jesus brings about what they signify— a move toward healing, well-being and wholeness.

Although Jesus did not formally institute this sacrament, it is rooted in his life and ministry. He healed people through concrete things and words: a smear of mud for a blind man, a touch for a leper and a bent-over woman, spit for a mute man, a splash of water for another blind man, the words "Little girl, arise" for a dead child, and "Courage, child, your sins are forgiven" for a paralytic.

Before ascending to heaven, Jesus told his apostles that those who believe and use his name "will cast out demons" and "will lay their hands on the sick, and they will recover" (Mark 16:17–18).

AN ACT OF THE CHURCH

There are many ways that the Anointing of the Sick is an act of the Church. A priest is the minister of the sacrament. Its graces ultimately come from Jesus, but the prayers and good works of all the Church members fortify the sick person as well. This is the meaning of the Church as the communion of saints. We are so united in Christ that where one member suffers, we all suffer. In addition, there is a symbiotic relationship among all of us. While the Church supports the sick person, in turn he or she can offer his or her sufferings to God for the benefit of all Church members and indeed all of humanity.

It is fitting that during the Anointing of the Sick a number of people are present to pray for and support those being anointed. In fact, *The Catechism of the Catholic Church* calls the Anointing of the Sick "a liturgical and communal celebration," whether it takes place in a home, hospital, nursing home or church, and whether it is celebrated for a single sick person or a whole group of sick persons. The faith of the entire community is required for the celebration of the sacrament. The presence of others shows that those suffering are not alone and that many people care about them in their time of need. (If it isn't possible to gather a group, the Church is still present in the persons of the priest and the one being anointed.)

WHO MAY CELEBRATE THE SACRAMENT

Baptized Catholics are encouraged to ask for the sacrament of the Anointing of the Sick as soon as they are "in danger of death." This does not mean that death is imminent but rather that the person's age or health puts them at risk.

Today's practice anoints people when they are:

- ill in any life-threatening way,
- depressed or mentally ill,
- weakened by advanced age,
- facing major surgery.

Common sense says that we don't celebrate the Anointing of the Sick for minor things—a bad cold or a broken arm, for example. On the other hand, the Church's policy is that if you are in doubt, you should request the sacrament. The priest will let you know if he thinks you are overusing it.

I know that my Redeemer lives,
And that at the last he will stand upon the earth;
and after my skin has been thus destroyed,
then in my flesh I shall see God.

Job 19:25–26

WHEN AND WHERE TO CELEBRATE THE SACRAMENT

The Anointing of the Sick is not meant to be a once-in-a-lifetime event. It may be received many times and certainly more than once. For example, a sick person who has already been anointed may become even sicker. Or a person may recover and then become ill again. An older person may become more and more frail. In all of these cases, repeating the sacrament is appropriate. Also, the sacrament is best celebrated early enough so that the ill person is alert and can more fully benefit from its prayers and comfort. It isn't necessary or even wise to wait until someone is on the brink of death before calling a priest

It used to be that the Anointing of the Sick conjured up the image of a priest anointing someone lying on the street after a terrible accident or in a hospital bed after a long illness. You can almost see the image of Bing Crosby as Father O'Malley finishing the anointing just as the person peacefully closes his or her eyes and "passes away." Today the sacrament is most often celebrated in a home and in church and long before someone is about to die.

If possible, the Anointing of the Sick should take place in the context of the Eucharist—the great sacrament of Christ's suffering, death and resurrection that is the source of power for all the other sacraments. This could happen at a special or a regularly scheduled Mass, during which one person or a whole group of people may be anointed. In a communal celebration of the sacrament, members of the parish stand with the sick against the illness. Songs about God's healing love enhance the ritual.

A home Mass is also appropriate if there is time and the person being anointed is able to participate. Otherwise, a simple receiving of Communion will tie the Anointing of the Sick with the Church's broader celebration of the Eucharist.

MANY GOOD REASONS
TO CELEBRATE THE SACRAMENT

If you've ever suffered from a toothache or a headache, you know how miserable and cranky it can make you. If you've ever had to care for a sick person, you probably know that sick people experience a bundle of negative emotions. They may feel lonely, depressed, useless, isolated, frustrated, discouraged, and jealous of the healthy. Used to taking care of themselves, they may deeply resent their weakness and dependence on others. On the spiritual plane, the sick may doubt that God loves them, forgives them, or even exists! Caretakers may be challenged by their patients' self-absorption, lack of interest, grumpiness, and suspicion of other people.

To complicate matters, if a person is near death, the struggle between good and evil often intensifies. Recall that in the Hail Mary we implore Jesus' mother to pray for us at the hour of our death and in the Our Father we ask that we be delivered from the Evil One.

Jesus, who is all compassion, sees us through these torments. His sacrament of the Anointing of the Sick strengthens us for the fight against suffering and evil, especially the final onslaught. Just as sickness affects our bodies, minds and spirits, the Anointing of the Sick remedies all three aspects of our being. Here are its wonderful effects:

1. The Holy Spirit bestows grace to endure and overcome the challenges of suffering and death. These graces are strength, peace and courage. Through the sacrament the sick or elderly person is gifted with strength to bear suffering bravely, combat illness, and fight temptation. Peace of heart dispels anxiety and turmoil, and the person becomes more patient and gentle. Courage and trust in God and his mercy replace fear, doubt, desperation and despair.

2. The person anointed receives the grace to unite himself or herself to the passion and death of Jesus. By bearing the cross gracefully, the person participates in redemption. This is the belief of Saint Paul who wrote, "Now I rejoice in my sufferings for your sake, and in my flesh I am filling up what is lacking in the afflictions of Christ on behalf of his body, which is the Church" (1 Colossians 1:24).

3. The suffering of the anointed one adds to the holiness of the Church. It is offered through Christ to the Father for the good of all people.

4. If this is the last anointing a person receives, it completes the good work begun by the anointings of Baptism and Confirmation. It fortifies the person for the final battles of earthly life before he or she is ushered into eternal life.

5. Anointing of the Sick takes away the remnants of sin, the punishment due for sin which is ordinarily removed by good deeds and acts of penance. In fact, if receiving the Sacrament of Penance is not possible, it also forgives sin directly, assuming the person is repentant.

6. In some cases the sacrament restores health, if this is for the spiritual good of the person. Our all-wise God might know that ultimately his or her suffering will lead the person to greater holiness, whether he or she recovers or not.

These effects of the sacrament are not dependent on the worthiness of the priest The results, however, are linked to the dispositions of the person receiving the anointing. Faith is essential. On the other hand, by infusing suffering people with greater faith and patience, the sacrament transforms them into witnesses to Christian hope. They become for us proclaimers of the Good News that through the mystery of Christ's suffering, death and resurrection our mortal life has been made new and will last forever.

HISTORY OF THE SACRAMENT

" " I am the LORD who heals you" (Exodus 15:26). This is how God iden-
tified himself to the Israelites. God says the same thing to us. The
actions of God the Son who walked our planet bear this out.

Teaching about Jesus, Saint Peter said, "He went about doing good
and healing all who were oppressed by the devil" (Acts of the Apostles
10:38). Jesus came to teach and to heal. "He cast out the spirits with a
word, and cured all who were sick. This was to fulfill what had been
spoken through the prophet Isaiah, 'He took our infirmities and bore
our diseases'" (Matthew 8:16-17). The Gospel recounts forty-one distinct
healings that Jesus performed and several references to his healing "all"
who were sick. He sent his apostles out to do the same: "Cure the sick,
raise the dead, cleanse the lepers, cast out demons" (Matthew 10:8). The
apostles obeyed. "They cast out many demons, and anointed with oil
many who were sick and cured them" (Mark 6:13).

After Pentecost, the apostles continued to work many signs and
wonders. In the Acts of the Apostles we read, "They even carried out the
sick onto the streets, and laid them on cots and mats, in order that Peter's
shadow might fall on some of them as he came by. A great number of
people would also gather from the towns around Jerusalem, bringing
the sick and those tormented by unclean spirits, and they were all cured"
(Acts 5:15–16).

The most convincing Scripture passage that the anointing of the
sick was integral to the life of the early Church is the following from a
first-century letter by one of its main leaders, Saint James:

*Are any among you sick? They should call for the elders of the
church and have them pray over them, anointing done with oil*

in the name of the Lord. The prayer of faith will save the sick, and the Lord will raise them up; and anyone who has committed sins will be forgiven.

James 5:14–15

For eight hundred years the Anointing of the Sick was viewed as a means to restore the sick to health. Although records are scant, it seems that the oil was blessed by the bishop and used to anoint the sick by presbyters (priests) and lay ministers alike. Prayer and the laying on of hands were part of the rite. There is even some evidence that oil might have been given internally like medicine, as well as used to anoint externally.

Somehow during the ninth century, the sacrament was transformed into a ritual that prepared people for death—removing their sins and strengthening them for their final battle. Through the influence of the emperor Charlemagne, the anointing was reserved to priests alone. The five senses (eyes, ears, nose, mouth, hands) were to each be anointed, and a prayer about the forgiveness of sins was said with each of these anointings—further associating the sacrament with the Sacrament of Penance. Finally, in the twelfth century, the Anointing of the Sick became known as Extreme Unction, "the final anointing," and it was administered after the sacraments of Penance and Viaticum (last Communion) for a dying person. These three became known as the "Last Rites."

The Church's Council of Trent in the sixteenth century affirmed that anointing the sick was a sacrament—one of seven listed by Peter Lombard, a twelfth-century theologian and bishop—and took steps to return the sacrament to its original intention. The Council decreed that the anointing should be given to those in danger of death, *especially* the dying, implying that it could be given on other occasions. The bishops at the Council also named the sacrament's effects: taking away sin and its remnants, strengthening the sick or dying person spiritually, and restoring health if it would benefit the person. They still insisted that only priests should administer the sacrament, which remains the rule today.

Despite this Council of Trent's interpretation of the sacrament as being for anyone who was sick, however, the majority of the faithful still saw (and feared) it as strictly for the dying. The Second Vatican Council (1962–65) changed the name of the sacrament to "The Anointing of the Sick" and stressed even more strongly that it was not only for the dying. It also changed the order for the administration of the last sacraments to penance, anointing, and Viaticum so that the anointing was no longer the last rite to be performed. Then in 1972 Pope Paul VI issued the *Rite of Anointing and the Pastoral Care of the Sick*, which shaped the sacrament pretty much as we celebrate it today.

If there be a true way that leads
to the Everlasting Kingdom, it is most certainly
that of suffering, patiently endured.

Saint Colette

SIGNS AND SYMBOLS

Because we are human beings gifted with five senses, we delight in using concrete things, gestures and words to convey ideas: A flag stands for a country, a handshake means friendship, and a heart symbolizes love. Depending on its color, a crossed ribbon can say "Fight AIDS," "Fight breast cancer," or "Support our troops." To mark events we create rituals that incorporate signs (things that point to something else) and symbols (things that stand for other things). Think of the signs and symbols surrounding a birthday, a wedding, or a holiday like Christmas or Easter. The songs, traditions, foods and colors for these special occasions reinforce what we are celebrating and add to the festivity.

Jesus knew how people worked. In his sacraments, signs and symbols speak to us about what is happening. In the words of Saint Augustine, sacraments are "a visible sign of an invisible grace."

OIL: ANOINTED FOR GLORY

The most obvious sign or symbol in the Anointing of the Sick is oil. The sacrament's old name, Extreme Unction, also focused on oil. The many uses of oil endow it with layers of meaning in the sacrament:

- Oil is fitting for this sacrament mainly because it is used for healing. Balm, salve, and ointments sooth and heal tired, wounded, aching and aged bodies.
- Oil tones the muscles of athletes and moisturizes dry skin.
- In cosmetics, oil makes people look better, healthier.
- Oil is related to food, our source of life. We not only consume oil, but we cook with it.

If God causes you to suffer much,
it is a sign that he has great designs for you,
and that he certainly intends to make you a saint.

Saint Ignatius Loyola

- Oil also gives us light. Recall that in Jesus' parable the five wise bridesmaids who had enough oil for their lamps were allowed to enter the kingdom (see Matthew 25:13).
- During Jesus' time, bodies were prepared for burial by anointing them with oil.

Oil has always been a sign or symbol of abundance and joy. In the Good Shepherd psalm, we pray, "You anoint my head with oil; my cup overflows" (Psalm 23:5). Found in all four Gospels is the story about a woman who pours precious oil on Jesus as a token of her love and esteem.

Moreover, the Israelites used oil to consecrate their prophets, priests and kings. Through these anointings, the Holy Spirit came upon them and prepared them for their special mission. The words *Christ* and *Messiah* mean "the one who has been anointed." Jesus, the Anointed One, has been anointed prophet, priest and king.

Formerly in the administration of the sacrament of the Anointing of the Sick, olive oil was always used. Now oil from any plant is acceptable. The oil of the sick (along with the oil of catechumens and chrism used in Baptism and Confirmation) is consecrated by the bishop of the diocese at the Chrism Mass on Holy Thursday morning. The oil becomes holy by God's blessing. Each parish keeps these holy oils in a special place in church called an *ambry*. If a priest administering the Anointing of the Sick is not able to use this oil of the sick, he blesses other oil before the anointing.

The priest anoints the person by making the Sign of the Cross with the oil on the forehead and on each hand. The oil of the sick marks a person for a future life of glory, which results from following Jesus, the Anointed One who bore the cross for us.

LAYING ON OF HANDS: SOLIDARITY

Touch is essential to human health. We know that babies who are held often and regularly are healthier and happier than those who are not. Sometimes a touch—a pat on the back, a squeeze of the hand or a hug—can lift us from the depths of sadness onto cloud nine. Jesus healed people by touching them and by letting them touch him.

Before the anointing, in silence the priest puts his hands on the person's head. This symbolizes the calling down of the Holy Spirit and the blessing and prayers of the Church, whose members are united with the person. The laying on of hands is a tangible sign of others' love and concern.

WATER: LIFE

Water is a strong sign of life and death: We absolutely need water to stay alive, yet it can also cause death, as the tsunami in Southeast Asia and the floods in New Orleans demonstrated. Because of its dual symbolism, water is used in Baptism, where we are first plunged into the death and resurrection of Jesus and then emerge to new life. To begin the sacrament of the Anointing of the Sick, the priest may sprinkle the person with holy water. He does this in remembrance of Baptism, when the person's life with Christ began.

WORDS: MEANING

During the anointing of the forehead the priest prays, "Through this holy anointing may the Lord in his love and mercy help you with the grace of the Holy Spirit. Amen." While anointing the hands he prays, "May the Lord who frees you from sin save you and raise you up. Amen."

The words used in the Anointing of the Sick send the message loud and clear that our God is a saving God. Did you know that the very name of Jesus means "God saves"?

The prayer of the sick person is his or her patience and acceptance of the sickness for the love of Jesus Christ. This has great worth when it is motivated by the imitation of how much He suffered for us, and by penance for our sins.

Saint Charles of Sezze

THE RITE OF THE ANOINTING OF THE SICK

What actually happens at the anointing of the sick? The service is simple and offers options that allow the priest to simplify it even more. Here is the basic outline:

1. The priest greets the sick person and others. If Communion is to be given, he places the Blessed Sacrament on a table where all can see and honor it.

2. The priest sprinkles the sick person and those present with holy water. He may say, "Let this water call to mind your baptismal sharing in Christ's redeeming passion and resurrection."

3. The priest instructs everyone on the meaning of the sacrament and perhaps says a short, spontaneous prayer.

4. The sick person may celebrate the sacrament of Penance while others leave the room. Otherwise all join in a general penitential rite, asking for forgiveness for themselves and for the sick person.

5. A brief Scripture passage is read, and the priest may comment on it.

6. Often at this point a litany for the sick is prayed by the priest, with response from those assembled, asking the Lord to help the sick person.

7. The priest lays his hands on the sick person's head. This is done in silence, letting the rich sign speak for itself.

8. The priest says a prayer of thanksgiving over the oil (or blesses it). Then he anoints the sick person on the forehead (or if this isn't possible, another part of the body) praying, "Through this holy anointing may the Lord in his love and mercy help you with the grace of the Holy Spirit. Amen." Then he anoints the person's hands, praying, "May the Lord who frees you from sin save you and raise you up. Amen." (Depending on the circumstances, one anointing may be sufficient.)

9. The priest prays for the person.

10. All pray the Lord's Prayer.

11. The sick person (and others present) may receive Communion.

12. The priest blesses everyone.

VARIATION

The Anointing of the Sick can take place during a communal celebration of the Mass at church. The priest wears white vestments and usually celebrates the Mass for the Sick. The anointing occurs after the homily, during which the priest speaks about the significance of anointing.

There can also be a communal liturgical celebration outside of a Mass. There may be a penitential rite. The Word of God can be celebrated with one or two readings and perhaps a song and short homily. The priest can address those who are sick and their loved ones. Then comes the laying on of hands, with the celebrant and every priest present imposing his hands over the sick individually. The anointing takes place, followed by the prayer after anointing and/or the Lord's Prayer. A litany for the sick is prayed before or after the anointing. The service ends with a blessing.

The next chapter explains how the rite is adapted for those who are dying.

You say that you are weak?
Have you fathomed the strength of God?

Saint Madeleine Sophie Barat

THE LAST RITES

Saint Joseph is the patron of the dying, partly because we assume that Jesus was with him when he died. The presence of his son would have guaranteed that Joseph had a happy death. Thanks to the sacraments, we too can have Jesus at our deathbed. The final sacrament we receive is our last Communion, called *Viaticum,* which means "with you on the way." Equipped with Viaticum as our provision, we can walk the final moments of our life's journey united with Jesus.

Ideally, a person near death is supported by three sacraments: Penance, Anointing of the Sick, and Viaticum—in that order. The Last Rites produce a plenary indulgence for the dying. This indulgence confers on the sick person the forgiveness of all sins and any punishment due them. The priest announces the indulgence at the end of the Sacrament of Penance or during the penitential rite at the beginning of Viaticum.

If the three sacraments that comprise the Last Rites are all celebrated, this is the procedure:

- The priest prepares the sick person for the sacraments.
- He hears the person's confession and/or has everyone join in a penitential rite.
- The plenary indulgence for the dying is given, which removes all punishment for sin that remains.
- The person renews his or her baptismal profession of faith.
- All pray a litany for the person.
- The sacrament of the Anointing of the Sick is conferred.
- Viaticum is celebrated and Communion is consumed.

Sometimes the sacrament of Confirmation is also needed. If so, in this case a priest may administer it. He does so before the blessing and prayer over the oil. Since Confirmation already includes the laying on of hands, this action is omitted in the anointing rite.

VIATICUM

Viaticum is so important that in urgent cases a person is given it without the anointing or before the anointing. It is fitting that we receive Communion at the hour of death. This sacred bread is called "the pledge of resurrection" because Jesus promised, "I am the living bread that came down from heaven. Whoever eats of this bread will live forever" (John 6:51). So important is Viaticum that it is the only one of the three "last sacraments" that is obligatory whenever it is possible.

The rite of Viaticum is a streamlined version of Communion within Mass. A Scripture text may be read. Then, before receiving Viaticum, the sick person renews his or her baptismal profession of faith by answering "I do" to the priest's questions. A litany for the sick person may be prayed. After the Lord's Prayer, the sick person receives Communion. Immediately after, the priest says, "May the Lord Jesus Christ protect you and lead you to eternal life." Others may also receive Communion. (The ordinary fast before Communion is waived for all.) After a concluding prayer, the rite ends with a blessing for those present. Then everyone may bestow a sign of peace on the sick person.

If the dying person isn't able to receive Communion under the form of bread, it may be given in the form of wine, even if it is only a drop. (Be sure to notify the priest before he comes if this is the situation.) Viaticum during a Mass may be received in the forms of both bread and wine.

A WORD ON DEATH AND RESURRECTION

For those who lack faith, death is a tragedy, because they think that a person simply vanishes into oblivion. But for those who believe in the promises of Jesus—who said, "I am the resurrection and the life," (John 11:25)—death is the birth into a new life of indescribable joy.

Every illness is a reminder of our inevitable death someday, but Catholics believe that death is not a period but a comma. It's the final act of life on earth, by which we complete our pilgrimage and make the transition into eternal life. No one escapes this doorway to our final destination, not even Jesus himself. Catholics also believe that the Blessed Mother was assumed body and soul into heaven. Her experience is a precursor to our own "resurrection of the body," which we profess in the Apostle's Creed. This belief emphasizes the sacredness of our physical bodies.

Those who are privileged to experience the sacraments of Penance, the Anointing of the Sick, and Viaticum at their death are completing this last rite of passage in grand style, prepared for eternal life in glory. Their earthly life ends accompanied by the power of the Risen Lord. With him they pray, "Father, into your hands I commend my spirit" (Luke 23:46). With him they achieve the ultimate triumph of life over death. They go on to live as they've never lived before.

This is the goal Saint Paul hoped for: "I want to know Christ and the power of his resurrection and the sharing of his sufferings by becoming like him in his death, if somehow I may attain the resurrection from the dead" (Philippians 3:10–11).

Anyone who bears sufferings with patience
for God's sake
will soon arrive at high perfection.
That person will be master of the world,
and will already have one foot in the other world.

Blessed Giles of Assisi

QUESTIONS ABOUT
THE ANOINTING OF THE SICK

M any people have questions about how the sacrament of the Anointing of the Sick is carried out, who may celebrate it, and related concepts. Not knowing the answers, they may hesitate to request the sacrament for themselves or propose the sacrament when it would be beneficial to someone they love. Following are the answers to some of these questions to help you facilitate the use of this consoling sacrament.

1. Why do good people have to suffer?

There are times when good people and innocent children suffer excruciating and perhaps long-lasting pain. We wonder about the justice of this. There is no answer. We must simply trust God's wisdom and his love for us and believe that the suffering can become redemptive when united to Christ's.

2. Why isn't everyone healed by the Anointing of the Sick?

Healing takes many forms. Someone who may not recover physically after the anointing may be healed in other ways. God knows what is best for everyone. We trust him to make the right decisions in our regard. In imitation of Jesus in the garden facing his death, all our prayers of petition ought to include the phrase, "not my will but yours be done" (Luke 22:41).

3. What if you aren't healed?

If you aren't healed, don't take it as a sign that your faith isn't strong enough or that God doesn't like you. You can identify with Saint Paul who wrote: "A thorn was given me in the flesh, a messenger of Satan to torment me, to keep me from being too elated. Three times I appealed to the Lord about this, that it would leave me, but he said to me, 'My grace is sufficient for you, for power is made perfect in weakness.' So, I will boast all the more gladly of my weaknesses, so that the power of Christ may dwell in me.... For whenever I am weak, then I am strong" (2 Corinthians 12:7–10). Do not become discouraged. Continue to pray and fight the pain. Trust in God for the grace you need to endure and come out victorious. Don't waste your suffering, but offer it up for others and for good intentions.

4. How can I help my loved ones accept the need for and get the most out of the Anointing of the Sick?

This might involve educating them about the meaning and benefits of the sacrament—especially if they have pre-Vatican II attitudes and see it only as part of the Last Rites. You may be the one who has to propose that the Anointing of the Sick be considered and arrange for it to happen.

5. How should I prepare for the reception of the Anointing of the Sick at home?

Near the sick person prepare a table by clearing it and covering it with a white cloth as a sign of reverence for the Blessed Sacrament. For atmosphere, you might set a cross and one or two lighted candles on the table. A glass or bowl of water for the priest to clean the oil off his fingers is helpful. If the person receiving Communion might have trouble swallowing the sacred host, it's a good idea to have a glass of water and teaspoon nearby.

6. Should the oil be wiped off after the anointing?

No, leaving the oil on the person reinforces its healing symbolism.

7. Can children receive the Anointing of the Sick?

Children who are seriously ill may receive the sacrament if they understand it enough to be comforted by it.

8. Can people who are mentally ill receive the Anointing of the Sick?

Those who have a serious mental illness and are capable of understanding and being strengthened by the sacrament may receive it. A doctor might be consulted to determine whether or not the sick person would benefit from the sacrament.

9. Can a person who has lost consciousness or the use of reason be anointed?

If it is reasonable to conclude that a person would have requested the sacrament if he or she were in control of their faculties, then it may be administered.

10. Can a person receive the Anointing of the Sick for alcoholism?

Inasmuch as this addiction is a threat to the life and well-being of the person, yes. The sacrament may especially help in the treatment stage, when the person often suffers most intensely.

11. Do priests anoint people who have already died?

No. This would be like giving medicine to a dead person. The deceased are beyond recovery. The priest can ask God to forgive their sins and receive them into the kingdom. However, if there is any doubt that a person is dead, the priest may administer the sacrament conditionally.

12. Since we all need inner healing, why doesn't everyone receive the Anointing of the Sick whenever it's offered?

This sacrament is specifically intended for those who are very ill physically. To broaden its scope to include everyone would demean its purpose and sign value.

13. Can laypeople anoint?

Although today priests are the sole proper ministers of the sacrament of the Anointing of the Sick, laypeople may anoint others with blessed oil in a nonsacramental rite. Their faith and prayers may comfort the sick person and possibly bring about a cure.

14. What is the procedure if someone brings Communion to a sick person at home?

Prepare a table covered with a linen cloth for the Blessed Sacrament. You might also provide candles, a crucifix, and holy water. Meet the priest or extraordinary minister of the Eucharist at the door and escort him or her to the sick person. The service may include a penitential rite, reading from Scripture and the Lord's Prayer. Then the priest or extraordinary minister shows the Eucharist and say, "This is the Lamb of God who takes away the sins of the world. Happy are those who are called to his supper." The sick person and all who are to receive Communion say, "Lord, I am not worthy to receive you, but only say the word and I shall be healed." Then Communion is given, followed by a period of silence. The priest or extraordinary minister prays a concluding prayer and blesses everyone.

15. What should we do after the Anointing of the Sick?

After the sacrament is received, offer a prayer of thanks to God for the sacrament and its solace. If the person improves or recovers, you might suggest celebrating a Mass or saying some special prayers together in thanksgiving.

It is suffering that makes us like to Him.

Saint Thérèse of Lisieux

SCRIPTURE READINGS FOR THE ANOINTING OF THE SICK

Here are a few Scripture passages related to the Sacrament of the Anointing of the Sick. Read each one thoughtfully and ponder its meaning for you and your life. The passage might prompt you to make a resolution. If so, record it on page 64. From time to time reread your resolutions and see to what extent you are keeping them.

JESUS CARES FOR THE SICK

A man was going down from Jerusalem to Jericho, and fell into the hands of robbers, who stripped him, beat him, and went away, leaving him half dead. Now by chance a priest was going down that road; and when he saw him, he passed by on the other side. So likewise a Levite, when he came to the place and saw him, passed by on the other side. But a Samaritan while traveling came near him; and when he saw him, he was moved with pity. He went to him and bandaged his wounds, having poured oil and wine on them. Then he put him on his own animal, brought him to an inn and took care of him. The next day he took out two denarii, gave them to the innkeeper, and said, "Take care of him; and when I come back, I will repay you whatever more you spend." Which of these three, do you think, was a neighbor to the man who fell into the hands of the robbers?" He said, "The one who showed him mercy." Jesus said to him, "Go and do likewise."

Luke 10:30–35

Saint Augustine interpreted this parable of the Good Samaritan as a story about Jesus and the human race. Like the man on the journey we have been attacked by Satan, stripped of our supernatural gifts, and left to die. Jesus comes along and in his compassion binds up our wounds and heals us. He takes us to the inn (the Church) and donates money (grace) so we continue to get care for our ills. The care given us is the sacraments.

The common interpretation of the parable is the one Jesus intended when he told it. We are to be merciful to anyone who is in need, especially the sick, even if the person is our enemy. Whereas the first two travelers are too busy or too self-absorbed to stop, the Samaritan interrupts his trip and goes out of his way to help the suffering man. Compassion compels him to use his own possessions in caring for the victim: his cloth, oil, wine, as well as his money. He even offers to return and pay more if necessary. This is the extraordinary kindness to the sick that Jesus expects of his followers.

JESUS HEALS PETER'S MOTHER-IN-LAW

As soon as they left the synagogue, they entered the house of Simon and Andrew, with James and John. Now Simon's mother-in-law was in bed with a fever, and they told him about her at once. He came and took her by the hand and lifted her up. Then the fever left her, and she began to serve them.

Mark 1:29–31

One of Jesus' first miracles of healing was for a family member of Simon (whose name Jesus later changed to Peter). When Jesus goes into Simon's house, people tell him that Simon's mother-in-law is sick. When our relative or friend is sick, we too need to tell Jesus and count on his help. Through our intercession for the person at Mass and in our daily prayers, Jesus will hear and come.

Jesus came to Simon's mother-in-law and by his touch raised her from her sickbed, in the same way he will someday raise us all at the end of the world. In Luke's Gospel Jesus "rebukes" the fever, just as he rebukes Satan in people who are possessed. This shows his command over evil. Then when the sick woman is well again, she waits on the visitors. Her recovery enables her to continue to do acts of charity, and our good health should spur us to do the same.

The reign of life has begun; the tyranny of death is ended.
A new birth has taken place, a new life has come,
a new order of existence has appeared,
our very nature has been transformed.

Saint Gregory of Nyssa

OTHERS HEAL IN JESUS' NAME

One day Peter and John were going up to the temple at the hour of prayer, at three o'clock in the afternoon. And a man lame from birth was being carried in. People would lay him daily at the gate of the temple called the Beautiful Gate so that he could ask for alms from those entering the temple. When he saw Peter and John about to go into the temple, he asked them for alms. Peter looked intently at him, as did John, and said, "Look at us." And he fixed his attention on them, expecting to receive something from them. But Peter said, "I have no silver or gold, but what I have I give you; in the name of Jesus Christ of Nazareth, stand up and walk." And he took him by the right hand and raised him up; and immediately his feet and ankles were made strong. Jumping up, he stood and began to walk, and he entered the temple with them, walking and leaping and praising God.

Acts of the Apostles 3:1–8

Filled with the Holy Spirit, Peter cures the man lame from birth in the name of Jesus. In ancient times, knowing someone's name was synonymous with having power over him or her. For those who believe in Jesus, his divine power is unleashed through their words and actions. The leaders Jesus chose to guide his Church are channels of his grace and love to all through the gifts of the sacraments.

This is the first miracle account after the Holy Spirit comes upon the Church at Pentecost. In Acts 2:43 we read that the apostles awed everyone by "wonders and signs." This healing of Peter is one of those wonders, and it is similar to Jesus' healings. Notice the parallels to the healing of Peter's mother-in-law: the taking by the hand, the raising up, and the immediate results.

The man's healing is instant, and he just doesn't walk but leaps for joy. What the lame beggar has received far surpasses the value of silver and gold. His first response is to praise God, and he joins Peter and John as they go to the temple for prayer. Likewise, our first impulse when someone recovers (including ourselves) ought to be to praise and thank God.

SAINT JOHN SEES THE FUTURE

See, the home of God is among mortals.
He will dwell with them as their god
They will be his people, and God himself will be with them;
He will wipe every tear from their eyes.
Death will be no more;
Mourning and crying and pain will be no more,
For the first things have passed away.

Revelation 21:3–4

The last book of the Bible says that there will be a new heaven and a new earth, in which God and human beings will intimately share life together. Sorrow will no longer exists; there will be only sheer joy and unalloyed bliss. The source of our joy will be God, whose love for us is tender, overwhelming and awesome.

What will heaven be like? No one knows. Saint Paul says, "No eye has seen, nor ear heard, nor the human heart conceived, what God has prepared for those who love him" (1 Corinthians 2:9).

A good death does honor to a whole life.

Petrarch

PRAYERS FOR THE SICK

PRAYER FOR PATIENCE
Father,
your Son accepted our sufferings
to teach us the virtue of patience in human illness.
Hear the prayers we offer for our sick brother/sister.
May all who suffer pain, illness, or disease
realize that they have been chosen to be saints
and now that they are joined to Christ
in his suffering for the salvation of the world.
We ask this through Christ our Lord. Amen.

A PRAYER FOR HEALTH
All-powerful and ever-living God,
the lasting health of all who believe in you,
hear us as we ask your loving help for the sick;
restore their health,
that they may again offer joyful thanks in your Church.
Grant this through Christ our Lord. Amen.

PRAYER FOR AN ELDERLY PERSON

All praise and glory are yours, Lord our God,
for you have called us to serve you in love.
Bless all who have grown old in your service
and give N. strength and courage
to continue to follow Jesus your Son.
We ask this through Christ our Lord. Amen.

PRAYER BEFORE SURGERY

God of compassion,
our human weakness lays claim to your strength.
We pray that through the skills of surgeons and nurses
your healing gifts may be granted to N.
May your servant respond to your healing will
and be reunited with us at your altar of praise.
Gant this through Christ our Lord. Amen.

PSALM VERSES

These psalms may comfort those who are sick and help them express their thoughts and feelings to the Lord.

Psalm 23 The well-loved Good Shepherd psalm.

Psalm 102 This lament expresses the anguish of a sick person.

Psalm 116 A prayer of dependence on the Lord in time of distress.

Psalm 131 A song of quiet trust.

Psalm 139 In praise of God's saving presence.

Psalm 146 Praise for God's help.

SCRIPTURE READINGS

These Scripture readings may hearten the sick and dying. Any passages about Jesus healing people would also be consoling.

Matthew 11:28–30 Jesus invites us to find rest in him.

Luke 7:18–22 Jesus' many cures proves he is the promised Messiah.

Mark 16:15–18 Jesus' followers have power to heal.

Luke 9:23–26 The followers of Jesus must take up their cross.

Matthew 14:22-33 Jesus has power to calm the storms in our lives.

John 14:1-3 Jesus has a place prepared for us.

John 6:53–58 Those who eat the living bread will live forever.

1 Corinthians 2:9 We can't imagine what God has prepared for us.

MANTRAS

These single Scripture verses and short prayers are a comfort to the sick. Repeated over and over as calming mantras, they heighten the awareness of God's loving presence.

Who will separate us from the love of Christ? (Romans 8:35)

Whether we live or whether we die, we are the Lord's. (Romans 14:8)

I believe; help my unbelief! (Mark 9:4)

The Lord is my shepherd, I shall not want. (Psalm 23:1)

Whoever believes has eternal life. (John 6:47)

Even though I walk through the darkest valley,
I fear no evil; for you are with me. (Psalm 23:4)

To you, O LORD, I lift up my soul. (Psalm 25:1)

My soul thirsts for God, for the living God. (Psalm 42:2)

My Lord and my God! (John 20:28)

Lord Jesus, receive my spirit. (Acts 7:59)

I know only scientifically determined truth,
but I am going to believe what I wish to believe,
what I cannot help but believe.
I expect to meet this dear child in another world.

Louis Pasteur (of his dying daughter)

STATIONS OF THE CROSS FOR THE SICK

These Stations may be prayed for the sick. If you are sick, you can pray them for yourself by substituting words such as "me" and "my" for "the sick."

1ST STATION – JESUS IS CONDEMNED TO DEATH

O Jesus, hearing your verdict, you accepted your suffering and death. Give courage to those who are just hearing the news that they are sick. Help them be resigned to their fate and ready to cope with what they will suffer.

2ND STATION – JESUS CARRIES HIS CROSS

Jesus, you took up your cross to make up for the sins of the world, including mine. Give the sick the grace to accept their cross of illness and offer it with you for the salvation of the world.

3RD STATION – JESUS FALLS THE FIRST TIME

O Jesus, your weakness caused you to fall. Be with those who are struggling with the cross of illness. Strengthen them to go on bravely.

4TH STATION – JESUS MEETS HIS MOTHER

O Jesus, Mary felt your pain keenly and suffered along with you. Help the family members and friends of the sick. Comfort them in their sadness and give them hope.

5TH STATION – SIMON HELPS JESUS CARRY HIS CROSS

Simon assisted you, Jesus, on your path of suffering. Send people to the sick to ease their pain and discomfort.

6TH STATION – VERONICA WIPES THE FACE OF JESUS

O Jesus, Veronica bravely performed an act of compassion, and you rewarded her with the image of your face on her veil. Bless the doctors, nurses, and caretakers of the sick. Draw them closer to you through their experiences.

7TH STATION– SECOND FALL OF JESUS

With your second fall, dear Lord, your pain increased. Give patience and peace to those who are depressed and frustrated by their illness.

8TH STATION – JESUS MEETS THE WOMEN OF JERUSALEM

Jesus, you told the women who felt sorry for you to weep for themselves and their children. Grant the sick the grace to be sorry for their sins and to trust in your mercy and love.

9TH STATION – THIRD FALL OF JESUS

O Jesus, again you collapsed under the cross on the rough road. Bring hope to the sick and raise them up.

10TH STATION – JESUS IS STRIPPED OF HIS GARMENTS

Jesus you underwent the indignity of being stripped naked and left the world with nothing. Help the sick endure any humiliations their illness entails, especially being dependent on others for their basic needs.

11TH STATION – JESUS IS NAILED TO THE CROSS

On the cross, suffering excruciating pain, you forgave your enemies. May the sick know the peace of your forgiveness especially in their last hour.

12TH STATION – JESUS DIES ON THE CROSS

Jesus, for love of us you died to heal us. May the terminally ill die praying, "Jesus, for you I die" and repeating your words, "Father, into your hands I commit my spirit."

13TH STATION – JESUS IS TAKEN DOWN FROM THE CROSS

Jesus, your lifeless body was removed from the cross by your friends and given to your mother Mary. Strengthen and comfort those who suffer the pain of losing a loved one. Give them faith in your promise of eternal life.

14TH STATION – JESUS IS LAID IN THE SEPULCHRE

Jesus, your body was laid in a tomb where it awaited new life. Infuse the sick who most need it with hope in your words, "I am the resurrection and the life. Those who believe in me, even though they die, will live." (John 11:25)

MY RESOLUTIONS

After reflection upon the graces provided
by the Anointing of Sick, I resolve the following:

_____
_____
_____
_____
_____
_____
_____
_____
_____
_____
_____
_____
_____
_____
_____
_____
_____
_____
_____
_____
_____
_____
_____